# LIFE
# OUT OF
# DEATH

# LIFE
## OUT OF
# DEATH

Meditations on the Easter Mystery

Hans Urs von Balthasar

Translated by Davis Perkins

Fortress Press          Philadelphia

**Library of Congress Cataloging in Publication Data**

Balthasar, Hans Urs von, 1905–

  Life out of death.

  Translation of: Leben aus dem Tod.
  Includes index.
  1. Death—Religious aspects—Christianity—Meditations. 2. Jesus Christ—Resurrection—Meditations. 3. Jesus Christ—Crucifixion—Meditations. I. Title.
BT825.B26513 1985    236'.1    84–48704
ISBN 0–8006–1821–1

1250I84    Printed in the United States of America    1–1821

# CONTENTS

# TRANSLATOR'S NOTE

In these three provocative meditations, noted European thinker and writer Hans Urs von Balthasar analyzes with penetrating insight that most pervasive and unfathomable reality of everyday life: death.

Drawing upon his rich knowledge of the human psyche and culture, von Balthasar explores the mystery of death as it manifests itself in the basic contradiction of wanting to create something enduring out of the transitory material of human life. He proceeds to show how Christianity resolves this contradiction and how the Easter mystery originating in the death and resurrection of Jesus is significant for Christians today.

While there is a great deal about these subjects that must necessarily remain mysterious, this is not the case with the author's seemingly recondite use of the term "abandonment" in the first meditation. Though he speaks of abandonment in art, life, and death in a variety of ways, some of which may strike the reader as peculiar, finally, he does not intend to endorse abandonment in the Stoic sense of "giving up," or "resignation." Rather, he evokes the meaning of abandonment conveyed by the German mystic tradition in the term *Gelassenheit,* which here implies "giving oneself over to something" or "losing oneself in a higher cause." It is in this sense that abandonment plays a role in the Christian commerce of securing life out of death.

Though quantitatively short, the original text was quite long in terms of tortuous Teutonic syntax. Hence it is with sincere gratitude that I acknowledge the kind assistance of Professor Albert Blackwell in eliminating a host of translation infelicities. Analogous to the book's life-out-of-death theological dynamic, a less dramatic (but no less pronounced) shift occurred in which (somewhat) lively English emerged out of (seemingly) deathly German prose, and Professor Blackwell was of enormous help in this respect. Minor editorial alterations were made in the English text to ensure smoother reading and to accommodate the broader ecumenical audience which deserves to hear clearly the important message von Balthasar has to deliver. I would like to dedicate this translation effort to Drew and Elizabeth Perkins, two very lively people in whose pleasant company the translation was executed.

D. P.

# I
## LIFE IN
# DEATH

Dying is the most commonplace and in individual cases the most incomprehensible of occurrences because it crushes and scatters to the four winds the little bit of meaning that has been laboriously accumulated in a life. The newspapers on every page contain death and funeral notices that the unaffected person does not heed. In the presence of the death of a treasured, beloved person, the entire meaning of that person's life is placed in brackets. This meaning is not absolute, but fragmentary at best. We see islands of meaning in an infinite sea of meaninglessness.

Our gaze is focused on the beyond; though all peeks behind the curtain, all speculation (spiritualism, the doctrine about the transmigration of souls, and anything else people may concoct), do not reveal the mystery. And materialism reveals still less. The chain of this fragmentary meaning stretches into the future through the hope that one day a totality will come out of it, and this hope is more than utopian. We must be satisfied with the fragmentary, but is there no contradiction there—that we know about something like meaning whose lineage cannot be traced?

We must first of all discuss this contradiction which pervades all human existence and which appears unresolvable on the purely human level. But when Christianity offers itself as salvation for humankind we must pay attention to what solution it offers to the final, unbearable contradiction. We will do this in a concluding third part. In between, however, in the middle part, the attempt should be made to find something in human existence with which the Christian solution can connect. For if there is not that, one cannot see how Christianity can tie into our existence. Certainly this starting point will first become visible and efficacious when that which is distinctively "Christian" itself emerges. Otherwise it remains exposed to dangerous misunderstandings.

# EXISTENCE IN CONTRADICTION

The small child opens large eyes to the world. What it perceives—forms, colors, sounds—it does not understand. The phenomena are neither concealed nor alien, because it cannot yet relate them to itself. The "I" is not yet developed; what it has in consciousness lies halfway between subject and object. The genuine wonder of all these wonders of earliest beginnings, however, is this: that one day the smile of the mother is recognized by the child as a sign of its being accepted in the world and that because it smiles back the center of its own "I" discloses itself. It finds itself because it was found. And because it found a "you," the many "its" by which it is usually surrounded can be incorporated into a relationship of familiarity. That holds true throughout the years because the child grows up in the safety of the family. When the unfamiliar occurs it is included in the sphere of the familiar if possible, otherwise it remains unnoticed. Nature and spirit are harmonious together.

Puberty brings one of the first questionings of this

harmony. The maturing person recognizes for the first time his solitariness as a person and experiences therewith a previously unknown loneliness. He knows himself to be elevated above the confines of pure nature and not simply a copy of a species like the animals. And with the discovery of his solitariness a more indefinite, still dreamlike horizon of total meaning opens itself to the young person, which corresponds to his personal being. But at the same time his sexual capacity matures, which initiates him into the life cycle of his species.

The first experiences of love will unconsciously be the attempt to unite the two. The thrill of the experience conceals for the time being the contradiction that emerges all the more flagrantly in the subsequent, inevitable disillusionment. The disillusioned feels not only defrauded by his partner but also deeply defrauded by his own nature. This requires of him (and will not cease throughout his life to require of him) that he inscribe something absolute on the surface of a transitory material.

This experience becomes acute when the young person asks what he wants to accomplish in his life. It is a question that someone like an artist experiences most consciously and thereby also most agonizingly, but even a mechanic, a farmer, or a shopkeeper perceives something of it. The person wants to create something lasting that will be exempt from the passage of time, to make an absolute statement which will be an expression of his personal uniqueness. Naturally one must sometimes do purely transitory things like decorate a hall for a banquet, and one can even put something of one's personality in such a thing. But the human yearning extends further; no one wants the work wherein he seeks to express himself totally to be inscribed in the purely transitory. Rather it should carry the imprint of a form "that no time and no power can disintegrate."

Nevertheless, everything earthly is drawn in the sand of the transitory. It is forever snatched up into irretrievability, as we see from the history of art. We may pick a few of the most eminent casualties: almost everything from Sappho, from Aeschylus and Sophocles; in music, many operas from Monteverdi, over twenty works from Bach, the Gastein Symphony of Schubert; in painting, everything Greek, much from the Roman, Leonardo da Vinci's *Last Supper* and Gozzoli's Pisa frescoes in the last world war, to which also the German Romantics fell victim; in architecture, so many ruins from Borobudur to Cluny, how many collapsed through earthquakes? How many more—like the Parthenon or the Great Sphinx—only survive phantomlike?

People who understood themselves to be building for their gods could destroy because they were conscious of being able to produce something better—and they did. In this respect, we have become impoverished, though we restore or rebuild destroyed Gothic arches so long as we have the money for it. In the East the same obtains, only more partially. This certainly does not mean that the artists of our age, unlike those of earlier times, can speak no valid word. They simply have it more difficult because the prefabricated products of technology, designed to be made in a day, make so great a claim upon the inventive and formative power of modern man that it becomes harder to make the binding word hearable and visible over it all. The great works of even our time prove, though, that the creative have not lost the courage to battle against the transitory.

Yet another contradiction in human existence besides that of art must be considered: we speak of its manifestation in "first love." It becomes striking in marriage, where marriage is still taken seriously. Two people decide to belong to each other "for life," but they decide this in view of an eternity, for they want to love each other absolutely. "For life" does not mean "I will love you as long as you live and after that I am again free." They mean the contradiction of an absolute inside bounded time.

Suppose one of them dies before the other. It is always a painful paradox when out of love the dying one releases the survivor: "You will remarry, won't you? Otherwise you'll be so alone. . . ."

But the highlighting of the contradiction that the person would like to—and even should—attain something permanent within the transitory is not yet the final word on the matter. The contradiction is not only unresolvable but also has a disturbing necessity—even fruitfulness. Georg Simmel and after him Max Scheler have explicated this: because my appointed time is finite, I can and must fashion something that is fully responsible. If we continue further into the incalculable, I can always countermand each of my decisions, everything is reversible, turning in circles. Meaning comes to term only when it moves upward in a direction toward a goal and termination point (one says: "in the sense of hands on a watch"; in French one says "sens unique" ["one way"] for a one-way street). And because I know myself free for a choice, for a work, for the love of a person, I affirm my knowledge of the uniqueness of my finite life.

I stare the contradiction of my existence in the eye, for I know that the stuff—whether the stuff with which I now work as a craftsman or the stuff of my diminishing hours—upon which I want to impress an absolute form will not withstand it. And with more perfect certainty it will be stripped from me in my final days.

At most what I can say then is this: in my brightest moments, in my positive decisions of consequence, I would like to make something lasting and valid of my existence—even though I know that most of my existence will disintegrate into dust and decay. Not only my biological but also my personal life—out of which I have tried to fashion something—ends. I see no way in which the problem may be solved. I do not, however, also want to claim to have done everything that I should have done. Would I not have landed at the same spot even in the event I had applied myself better?

Whatever kind of abysmal ignorance awaits us at the close of our life rules over it as a whole even more. We do not need to term it resignation; it is simply an ignorance—a sort of burning fire into which goes all we have undertaken to build. Should not the entire pervasive atmosphere be one of anxiety?

# ABANDONMENT

We do not want to leap over this hopelessness immediately into Christianity since this would be nothing other than a *deus ex machina*. Such could only come to us externally and from on high, and what sort of solution to the human contradiction would that be? The attempt to find direction within the finite must be ventured. We should be able to glimpse a dawn from which the glimmerings of an answer may shine.

Everyone who desires something absolute in life, whether it be a love or an accomplishment, must sacrifice himself. He must pay with himself for what he wants to buy. And likewise, when he wants to express himself as powerfully as possible, he must abandon himself for the sake of his expression.

The young person who sees before him thousands of possibilities for the realization of his life must make his selection. For what, when it becomes serious, do I want to renounce my thousand possibilities? For what do I want to sacrifice my all-powerful freedom, for it is now imperative to do the one thing necessary?

In his *Either/Or,* Kierkegaard described the not-wanting-to-decide existence—the "aesthetic"—with all the glamor of Mozart's Don Giovanni, who still remains only a dilettante at love and therefore is finally taken by the devil. The second stage on life's way, then, is that of a modest marriage which is nothing dazzling, rather only a soft glow from within—which others see as almost fortuitous. We don't yet need to speak here of the third, religious stage in Kierkegaard's "Stages on Life's Way." Remaining with the young person for the moment, he understands instinctively that in the choice of *one* reality from among a thousand possibilities lies not only the gravity of life but also the dignity of life. An instinct, an inner hearing inspires him to commit himself to a vocation, to choose a profession. And he must abandon himself to it.

We should say moreover that no one finds himself in any other way than through such actual self-abandonment. His self will not be comprehensible from the meditation mat. At most he will encounter nothingness as he abstracts himself from everyone, and it would be a pity if he wanted to recognize himself therein, for it is only in devotion to a thing or a person that this can be accomplished. The ability to abandon self is the principle underlying all achievement and all loving possession. "The work must be, though I perish in it!" "You must be, even if it costs me my life!" Great art will not be purchased otherwise. In vain the pope orders the one lost in his work finally to descend from his scaffolding to the floor of the Sistine Chapel. The artist's abandonment is no mere ruse for investing himself more deeply in his project, as becomes perfectly clear through the tenacity of his devotion.

We maintain, then, that this most beautiful and fruitful human attitude is what was meant in the German mystic tradition of the Middle Ages with the extolling of the term "abandonment" *(Gelassenheit)* and is what characterizes the most important art in life. In death we will forcefully be led from ourselves into total abandonment, because we will be commanded to abandon everything and ourselves.

Is there perhaps a way open for coaching us without constraint through this all-important act of life? The question is not at all easy to answer because we have the feeling that two completely different things would be asserted here. The first leads into the joy of possession through my striving, not for my own sake, but rather for the sake of another. The second robs me of every possession. From this potential ambiguity regarding being abandoned, a very dangerous path opens before us—namely, the attempt to make the two ways compatible. We must linger over this matter a moment.

Throughout the entire history of philosophy and otherworldly wisdom the teaching of the dying Socrates is repeated to us: philosophy or wisdom is finally nothing other than lifelong training in death. That can be true, but it can also be basically false. It is true where my most inward resolve for achievement and love is not bent back upon me, where I do not seek "self-realization," but rather where I seek the objective worth of the work or the person—and also seek to promote and foster this worth through my substance. Through my declining, the essential, which I intend, rises up. That can actually be the highest of all human, worldly wisdom, and this wisdom will confirm and complete the Christian wisdom over and beyond itself. But quite often the same maxim is also falsely understood and implemented: above all, where abandonment is conceived as a distancing from the transitory things or people, as a looking through to the inner nothingness of everything worldly and finite. That can have very different levels of intensity. Most intensive is Eastern wisdom, for which everything finitely limited is simply appearance and delusion, *Māyā*, illusion. Everything finitely limited (therefore even my own self) is such that it actually indicates only a desire to be and to have. Therefore even the world around me must be renounced. This alleged wisdom is today ever more fashionable and powerful among us. It is more seductive as it needs to point only to the contradiction in existence: it is *sūnyatā*, emptiness. Our self-seeking after abiding actualization is exposed as "thirst" *(trsna)*, which cannot be quenched other than through abolition of the desiring I, through attainment of selflessness (Sanskrit: *an-atman*, Japanese: *muga*).

Stoicism repeated this in a milder version. In Stoicism the four basic passions—pleasure and aversion, fear and yearning—should be eradicated from the soul so that in the stillness of the inner person *apatheia* can prevail (hence the word "apathy"). But can such a person still venture into a real activity or a genuine love?

The most subtle form is probably the Socratic-Platonic, which persuades us that one need no longer fear death because it is simply a matter of a foreign element, the temporal body, dropping away from us finally. Then, liberated from it, we can as immortal souls at last be unhampered. The German Enlightenment and German Idealism are full of this teaching: in death the butterfly flies out of the cocoon.

But also, the Stoics had an enduring influence upon Christian thought and sensibility—already on the church fathers, on the Middle Ages with its tracts on the vanity of the world, and most strongly on the baroque.

This manifold and yet concentric interpretation of abandonment is the most pernicious enemy not only of Christianity but of authentic humanity in general. This is because when seriously implemented it paralyzes every genuine involvement in earthly transitory life—in action as well as in love.

It is still not clear, however, how one can escape this interpretation, or, said another way, how commitment and abandonment may be united. That is a question about people as such, a humanistic question. Nevertheless a liberating response is given only by the Christian interpretation of life.

# CHRIST

One can meaningfully put the question in a Christian way: Did the Son of God become man in order to act or to die? Many church fathers—for example, Tertullian, Gregory of Nyssa, Leo the Great—have unhesitatingly answered: he was born in order to be able to die.

As long as he acted in life, his work remained a failure. The more he championed love, the more clearly he was rejected. Yet through his death on the cross he became the most formative figure in world history. Why so? The answer may be condensed into one sentence: Because his entire earthly action from the beginning resulted in total self-surrender to his heavenly Father and this self-surrender reached its zenith and thereby also its full impact in the cross.

In its brevity this answer sounds enigmatic, and in fact a notion is still missing that would allow us to understand it completely. Jesus said he did not come to do his will, but rather the will of the one who had sent him. And that was his nourishment. The missing notion is that of mission. With this notion we already glimpse from afar the sought-after unity.

Because Jesus, the Son of God, is only present in order to fulfill a divine commission in his actions and love, he will take this commission as seriously as possible. There can be no talk of an inner distancing from the commission.

But because Jesus had already always identified his total I with his mission, he had also abandoned it to the will of the Father. He could not retreat behind his mission in order to find his I or his self.

What does the mission consist of, though? It consists of his loving obedience which persisted to the very end and reconciled the world alienated from God to God. This is possible only because he takes this entire alienation as the eclipse of God upon himself and bears it through to the end—indeed, beyond the end—because his loving obedience to the Father is deeper and more definitive than any sinful rebellion can be. One may call the guilt of the world its lie and illusion, but the world itself, the human beings (upon which the mission of Jesus turns) are anything but *Māyā* and illusion.

His mission runs counter to the philosophical doctrine of dying. It is not a matter of detaching oneself from transitory things in order to escape into an actual or imaginary eternity, rather it is a matter of conversely allowing the seeds of eternity to be sown in the soil of the world and having the kingdom of God burst forth in this soil. The soil is as little an illusion as the human being; it is the genuine, realistic creation of God the Father which must now finally bear his fruit.

So it suddenly becomes clear: the Son of God comes with an absolute commission into this limited world, and the Father expects that this commission will be fulfilled unconditionally. Jesus is therefore exactly like any person in the situation of contradiction—the absolute should be resolved in the transitory. How is that possible? Only by his incorporating even his death (this hardest of all deaths) into his life's work so that in this passivity and negativity his entire positive and efficacious achievement completes itself, and by his moving toward this "hour" in which everything imperfect in this world will actually be perfected. What remains to be performed after his active life can no longer be shouldered by him; it can only be borne. And the necessity to bear an unbearable burden begins with the events on the Mount of Olives. Jesus must experience inwardly (without distancing himself from it) everything that alienated humanity in sin and anti-divine acts, so that he was literally "made to be sin" (2 Cor. 5:21) for us, according to Paul. Since this is the outright overtaxing of human ability, and Jesus (by virtue of the power of his obedience to the Father) is nevertheless the bearer of this burden, self-transcending action and passion so coincide that suffering is already dying.

The living body which accomplishes that is the most

elevated work of art and love in the world. In it the most hideous moment of our history in all its realism is transformed from within into the most beautiful. It is this enduring, forgiving, and transforming love that is appropriately conferred upon us as an abiding memorial in the sacrament of the Eucharist. It would not be what it is, though, if our dying was not also assumed in it and transformed in a feat of divine-human love. We drink the blood which was spilled through us, but, more deeply, for us. And if we fear death because we do not know how to die, though we accept that as a total entity one is snatched away, yet we should not forget that from the outset another has been able to do it for us—another who died not as an individual alongside us, but rather one who, suffering and dying, already assumed our death. He had already achieved the total devotion to the Father in his entire life, but in death he achieved this total devotion within our anxiety, our inability, and our insurmountable unwillingness. And he did this not for himself, but for us so that in the same act he transferred his entire achievement to us eucharistically.

His conscious achievement extends to the unity of atoning death and Eucharist. Everything else he entrusted to the Holy Spirit, who led him through life and whom he yielded up to the Father in death with his last breath. Jesus achieved the divine-human work of art and love, and he is not so artless as to interpret it himself also. Many modern exegetes do not understand that. They believe the speaking God (*Theos legon*) must also be his own theologian.

> I have yet many things to say to you, but you cannot bear them now. When the Spirit of truth comes, he will guide you into all the truth; for he will not speak on his own authority. . . . He will glorify me, for he will take what is mine and declare it to you. (John 16:12–13a, 14)

We attempt to bring our finite works to a conclusion ourselves. Jesus, though, did not need to explain the infinite work which he began and also completed, nor to make it palatable to the world. He could entrust it to the divine spirit for an open-ended interpretation. That is the highest Christian abandonment.

But it should not be forgotten that in this abandonment he is also left alone—that is, forsaken. "My God, why have you forsaken me?" In the God-forsakenness every trace of meaning is obscured; only the question and the cry are still possible. The path leads into hopelessness. The death that is died here is the most difficult imaginable (although in reality it is unimaginable). The light that shines in the incomprehensible darkness understands itself to be no longer within the darkness. But that it still shines at all is the result of his indissolvable obedience to the fatherly sun. It gives itself over to the Father's intangible, shaping hands.

How difficult our dying will be within the death of

Jesus is not decided by us. God can lighten our death on the basis of the difficult death of his Son, or he can graciously allow us to feel something of this difficulty also. He will collect us in his fatherly hands even when we feel ourselves forsaken in Jesus, when we apparently sink into a groundless abyss.

But what becomes of our earthly achievement, whatever it may have been? Insofar as we have devoted ourselves to it, in order to glorify not ourselves but rather God and to offer up that which we might have claimed for ourselves, to that degree something of us will endure in eternity. In the "new heaven and new earth" nothing will be lost that was done or suffered in genuine devotion. In the last book of the Bible the eternal Jerusalem is described for us: all the treasures of the world will be housed therein. But they will be more beautiful and more precious than here because God's grace will be complete in them—an aspiration we had wished to express, but which was not possible for us.

Here an aspect of the anticipated eternal life from the end of the Creed becomes visible to us. In a very mysterious and ethereal sense, to be sure, there will without doubt be a "vision of God." But certainly not as if we were to sit eternally in front of a play in which God revealed to us the depth of his being and power. That would not suffice to perfect the creature. Goethe said repeatedly, and not wrongly, that he expected from eternal life a heightening of human creativity, for a person is only happy when he can achieve, give, actualize.

What inexhaustible possibilities underlie the most exalted works of a creative soul, like that of Bach or Mozart! Through the perfect self-surrender of human nature in Christ's death (which seizes hold of our dying and conveys it to perfection) the powers of love and of achievement in our nature become free—powers that will unfold in God's eternity.

# II
# LIFE OUT OF
# DEATH

Our first meditation considered the residency of death in all of transitory life in a way which respected not only the fact that death impinges in every moment as the physical end of mortal life but the fact that it also bestows an unparalleled dignity in the spiritual dimension of our existence: the force of an irrepeatable uniqueness and the concomitant responsibility. This may not be one-sidedly construed as training in the business of gaining the necessary perspective on the earthly—that was the narrow understanding of abandonment. Rather it is at the same time readiness for the demand of the ever-unique moment which the seriousness of the mission brought into view. In both dimensions renunciation of living out one's life was a condition for truly living in one's life.

# THE POWER
# OF GOD

This still does not, however, take us beyond the irre-solvable paradox of human existence: needing to incor-porate the absolute into transitory matter. The only time Jesus wrote, he wrote in the wind-blown dust. And the paradox itself blows away as the posthumous fame, memory, and influence are sooner or later buried with us in a final death which turns us to dust. Christ himself was not willing and able to coordinate the total-ity of his earthly activity and suffering with its entire immanent significance; rather he turns it over to the invisible hands of God. And he does not take the spirit of his mission into death with him, but dying breathes it out and returns it back to the Father. So the entire aban-donment first completes itself: in being taken, in vol-untarily allowing oneself to be taken. "No one takes it [my life] from me, but I lay it down of my own accord" (John 10:18). Here death (and what a death!) appears as the highest, most vital achievement of life. On account of this achievement Jesus says "the Father loves me" (v. 17).

From this it does not now follow, however, that the final death which the person dies is less gravely death or that this vital achievement of allowing oneself to be taken removes the sting from death. Good Friday is not followed by Easter, but rather by the "descent into the underworld of the dead" in which, according to the Psalms, no one has the vitality any longer to praise God (Ps. 6:5). Death is a denial of all life and its functions. Therefore it is not nothing or plain annihilation, although in general we cannot envisage this life-denying state of affairs in which the body returns to the earth and life to the God who gave it (Job 34:14–15; Ps. 104:29; Eccl. 12:7). It is like an exhalation and inhalation of God.

And so it becomes clear that he alone, who is the source of all life, can infuse new life into death (which is not simply nothing). Sovereign, free, irrespective of the gains or losses of past life, he alone is the one "who gives life to the dead" (Rom. 4:17) in "the immeasurable greatness of his power . . . according to the working of his great might," as Paul, heaping up phrases, expresses himself (Eph. 1:19).

That applies to the raising of Christ "from the dead," and it applies likewise to us—not yet to physical death, but to spiritual death: "yield yourselves to God as men who have been brought from death to life" (Rom. 6:13b); "Arise from the dead, and Christ shall give you light" (Eph. 5:14). But this only because God first called his dead Son "from the dead" (Matt. 17:9; Luke

16:30–31, 24:46; John 20:9; Acts 3:15; 13:30; 17:5;
Heb. 13:20) back into his divine life.

And now the decisive thing. This new life that has
definitively put death behind itself (Rom. 6:10)
remains nevertheless life out of death, life characterized by its passage through death. It is life which on the
one hand has power over death ("I have the keys of
Death and Hades" Rev. 1:18), but on the other hand
remains profoundly marked by the event and experience of death insofar as this highest achievement of life
was—and remains—the same as total self-surrender.
Therefore one eternally looks upon the apocalyptic
lamb's character through death: he is living, but "as
though slain" (Rev. 5:6, 9, 12; 13:8). And because the
"lamb without blemish or spot . . . was destined [to be
slain] before the foundation of the world" (1 Peter
1:19b–20a), there is no reason why Rev. 13:8 may not
be translated: "the lamb, slain before the beginning of
the world." The one who was single-handedly to
receive power and judgment over the living and the
dead must necessarily also become acquainted with all
the human conditions, including that of death. The one
to whom "every knee should bow, in heaven and on
earth and under the earth [in the realm of death]" (Phil.
2:10), who should ascend "above all the heavens,"
must also pass through the places and conditions
"below the earth" in the realm of death (Eph. 4:9).
And from this supraheavenly, divine height, Christ not
only fulfills "his all" but also dispatches the churchly

missions shaped by him, which will be marked accordingly by his life unto death and by his life out of death.

If, however, death (from which God's power reclaimed the Son) is stamped with his eternal life, then also everything in the domain of death is necessarily stamped with the contribution made by his earthly life. And what in this life was not characterized by sacrifice and renunciation to the will of the Father! Above all, the event of the "hour of the Father" and "the darkness"—all phases of the passion, to whose transfigured participation in eternal life the stigmata revealed to the disciples bear witness. The most deathly of these wounds, the pierced heart, does not mend again in temporal life. Thomas, who lays his hand in the side, touches only the openness of this heart. Nothing of the sacrificed body and spilled blood is gathered together again in order to produce a living body according to our understanding. Rather the complete outpouring into death is the maximum vitality that could be attained on earth, and only in this form of final self-sacrifice does the corporeally resurrected one live his eternal life henceforth. And this not in a confused, diffused form that dissolves his own being; rather in a most definite lordship, impressing every area of the whole realm of his indwelling with his character of sonship. This character of sonship, however, can only be properly grasped in the trinitarian context. What appeared not yet clear to our dull eyes in their earthly form about the source, the Father, is now per-

fectly transparent to him. The blinding glory, for example, with which he appeared to the persecutor near
Damascus is the total fulfillment of all the appearances
of Yahweh's glory in the Old Covenant—to Isaiah, or
Ezekiel, or Daniel, none of whom lost physical eye-
sight from this glory as did Paul. "Who sees me, sees
the Father" is now no longer a paradox for us, but an
immediate reality. He still mediates, but within imme-
diacy: "I do not say to you that I shall pray the Father
for you; for the Father himself loves you" (John
16:26b–27a).

And as he introduces us into the depths of the Father,
so he breathes into us the Spirit who gives us the meaning and the heart with which we can enter into the eternal triune love. For "the Lord is the Spirit, and where
the Spirit of the Lord is, there is freedom" (2 Cor.
3:17)—the freedom of the family of God, who has
access in the Spirit through the Son to the Father. In the
resurrected son, his human nature secures immediate
participation in the triune life. This becomes most
clear where he no longer simply breathes the Spirit
together with God the Father, but with supreme con-
creteness breathes into the band of disciples in order to
give them the Holy Spirit and therewith the power for
forgiving sins (John 20:22).

But the resurrected one, especially according to
Luke and John, is also the perfection of humanity (in a
heavenly sense only). The words, gestures, and actions
derive from a tenderness that is not at all abstract or

dreamy, but rather totally near and promising. It leads
one down the passageway through death into a final
human experience that encompasses life. What is more
tender and more intimate than the words exchanged
with Mary Magdalene at the open grave? What is more
lovely than the conversation on the road to Emmaus
climaxing in the sharing of bread? What is at the same
time so intimate and so restrained as the breakfast by
the sea? And where it is possible to find fault because
faith is lacking, what is more gracious than that in
admonition there is always the gift of presence, indeed
of contact, as is most movingly implied in the first resurrection passage of John: in spite of being able to have
contact, being challenged to forgo it? Or the eluding of
Magdalene, in order that she might be given something
better, something more in the spirit of Easter: the trans-
mission of the good news about the resurrection to the
brethren?

But the most wonderful thing is perhaps this: that in
appearing to the disciples who had denied him and fled
disgracefully Jesus did not speak about his forgiving
them. Rather, passing over this, he places the ecclesiastical right to forgive in their hands as the product of
his cross: "Receive the Holy Spirit. If you forgive the
sins of any. . . ."

In the resurrected one, the God in him appears most
divine, and the human in him appears most human—
but both inseparably united. The divine grandeur manifests itself in such a way that he is only recognized

when he gives himself to be recognized. This is not estrangement from everyday, earthly realities, rather it turns itself immediately into the most trustworthy nearness. He gives peace to the fearful. That is, *his* peace that he brings forth from the cross, death, and the underworld—a peace in which the peace of death is transfigured as it is entered.

# THE DISSOLVED
# SUBSTANCE

The disciples owed the appearances of the Lord during the forty days primarily to his condescension. It gave them a humanly discernible proof that in life and suffering Jesus fulfilled every promise. But the Lord is concerned to emphasize the provisionality of these days. He cannot be held fast; he appears and fades away when he will. He refers one to faith and above all to that presence with which he endowed the Holy Communion and which should remain henceforth authoritative. By breaking bread in Emmaus and disappearing in the same moment he pointed to this abiding presence.

One can argue about whether the injunction to repeat "Do this in remembrance of me" was given before the suffering. But the fact that he himself as the resurrected one continued the meals and that the disciples understood themselves to be assembled for the breaking of bread (the understanding mediated to us first by Paul in 1 Corinthians 11) proves clearly that from the beginning the faithful understood Jesus' wish to remain in this way among them. In a similar way it is an effusive gift that the church is not only instituted by Jesus but also endued with self-responsibility—as on Easter evening, when it was endued with the authority to forgive sins in the Holy Spirit.

And if this Easter grace of absolution presupposes Jesus' cross and death, which in the death of abandonment is vicariously "made into sin," the institution of the Eucharist includes this same cross and this same death in anticipation within itself. Indeed, there the body in its broken form and the blood in its spilled form are offered for eating and drinking. How the living Lord in the form of corporeal solidity was able from the outset to make use of this corporeality in the dissolution of death remains his mystery. However, as in the transfiguration at Mount Tabor his divine sonship could manifest itself throughout the entire realm of his corporeality, so by virtue of his free self-sacrifice ("no one robs me of my life; I lay it down freely") he also has the power to control his condition of death. And this in a double sense: that in the form of his final sacrifice he makes himself into the food of those who belong to him, and that, as in the bestowal of the authority of absolution, he surrenders the administration of this most important form to those who belong to him, whom he "consecrates" with himself (John 17:19). In the parallel between the events of Maundy Thursday and those of Easter evening one sees how the self-sacrifice of Jesus can develop into a (co-)sacrifice of the church.

Both sacraments, Eucharist and confession, are unlike the other sacraments (which are primarily singular occurrences in the life of Christians) in that they pulsate rhythmically throughout this life. Both sacraments are life out of death. In confession the sinner who is dead for God is restored to a life through God and for God through the Lord, resurrected from the sinner's death. What was dead in him, the descending, dead Lord buried there in the underworld in order to permit it to be resurrected with him to the Father. "Arise from the dead!" (Eph. 5:14) the resurrected one calls to him as he had previously in the earthly symbol called the physically dead to life. The Eucharist, though, is placed before the passion and death in order to enable those participating in the mysterious meal to go together with the Lord into the final sacrifice: the surrender of the spirit into the Father's hands (Luke 23:46), which is in death simultaneously the highest achievement of the transmitted life. This achievement of Jesus is his faithful obedience to the Father in the power of the Spirit—an obedience that produces something from physical and even from spiritual death (in which the Father "forsakes" and the Spirit is "surrendered") that, beyond all deaths, but including their radicalism, produces a work of the Living One. Therefore "He who believes in me, though he die, yet shall he live, and whoever lives and believes in me shall never die" (John 11:25–26). The unrelenting, ensuing question—"Do you believe this?"—is the question of the Lord to the communing, who will never die because they are ready to die with the Lord.

This applies more especially to the celebrants who must speak the words with Jesus himself: "This is my blood shed for you and the many." But likewise these co-celebrants believe it and are therefore ready to die in order never to die.

Nowhere is the church so greatly extended beyond itself as here where it is grounded in its special way through the sacrament. Jesus dies for "the many," the "children of God scattered abroad" beyond Israel (John 11:52). There is no sinner for whom he did not vicariously die the death of sin in the divine remoteness. For this reason the Eucharist can only be celebrated "beyond the world" (as Teilhard says) no matter how in the present it produces the corporate body, which can understand itself only as existing for the (indeterminant) "many." The believing believe for the nonbelieving; the communing commune for the non-communing because the body that is received bore the sins of all. The sins of all are what killed Jesus. Had he not taken away from us that which is ours, he could not give us in its place that which is his (which is not on this account alien to us, as if it were an artful prosthesis) because that which is his assumes that which is ours in order to give it back to us transformed (from death to life). In its ecclesiastical particularity, however, this is intentionally a more universal process. It is the world that the Father intends to reconcile with himself through Christ's atoning death (2 Cor. 5:19).

One may never overlook the role of the Holy Spirit in this universalization (which does not abrogate particularity and personality). In contrast to the partial outpouring of the Holy Spirit to the prophets, the Holy Spirit reposed always in Jesus "not by measure" (John 3:34) and can be seen there on the cross where Jesus surrendered himself immeasurably and Jesus can pour out the Spirit immeasurably through time and space. The historical becomes panhistorical without thereby becoming non- or transhistorical. This is visible in Jesus' self-commitment to the eucharistic celebration that he entrusts to his bride the church, which stood under the cross in Mary and John—there pierced alive by the mortal sword where the heart of the dead Christ was pierced. Mary, the church "without blemish" (Eph. 5:27), is by his last will entrusted to her new son John and is thereby incorporated into the visible church which has its principle of unity in Peter. The community remains indissoluble between the pierced Jesus and his bridal "body" for all time. From this unity which cannot be dissipated as a part of any synthesis (of "churches" or of worldly organizations) the universalization of the holy results through the Spirit.

But it must further be remembered that this univer-salization is nothing other than life out of death. Because Jesus died not only his personal death but the death for all sinners—and thus for all—he incorporated the universal death into his personal vitalism. "I died, and behold I am alive for evermore, and I have the keys of Death and Hades" (Rev. 1:18). He has these keys because he himself was dead and in Sheol, but more-over because he bore the death of all in himself and therefore has the power over the whole of Hades. As his earthly life was polarized by this general death, so also his eternal life remains eucharistically polarized.

In this shape the eucharistic life of Jesus is ultimately also the ecumenical form of his trinitarian devotion to the Father—which he does not "have," but "is." If the will of the Father and the completion of his work were the enduring "eucharistic" food for the earthly Jesus (John 4:34), so all the divine hypostases are mutually "eucharistic" food in the inner trinitarian life.

Even the Father nourishes himself from the Son, without whom he could not be the Father. So also both are only Father and Son through the Holy Spirit. The Holy Spirit, however, is just as much "nourished" by both as "nourishment" for both.

This "losing" of self together and in each other can-not, however, be called death (or "emptiness," "noth-ingness"); rather it is the model and expression of greatest vitality. And from this mystery of divine life it

becomes possible that even the natural death of crea-
tures can be an image of God (which cannot be said of
the death of sin) and, all the more, that Jesus Christ can
impress something of the trinitarian life of devotion
upon worldly death.

# DYING IN
# SERVICE

Much of what has been said clarifies itself when one perceives the forty days of the resurrected one with his own as the time of the sending of the church into the world—but with the requisite presupposition of the formation of a church capable of mission. The church is basically a community of believers and participants in Christ. The sending, however, is the passing beyond this form of community into the isolation of the ever-individual mission. Indeed, the "charismata" permit themselves to be construed in the first place as functions within a community (quiet and integrated within itself). But this quiet is almost impatiently burst open by the resurrected one. "All authority [not simply in the church, but] in heaven and on earth has been given to me. Go therefore and make disciples of all nations, baptizing them . . . , teaching them to observe all that I have commanded you; and lo, I am with you always, to the close of the age" (Matt. 28:18b–20). "As the Father has sent me, even so I send you" (John 20:21b), not to Israel, not simply to the church, but to the area "outside"—for the shepherd goes outside before the sheep which he has "brought out" (*ekbalē*, John 10:4). This outside is the place where there are wolves who are not harmless, but "snatch" and "scatter" (John 10:12, Acts 20:29). But this is precisely the whither of the mission: "I send you out as sheep in the midst of wolves" (Matt. 10:16a).

Here the mission becomes deadly earnest. Mission, the center of the Christian life, presupposes a doubly affirmed death. One death is the death of the private person who no longer lives for himself and his own purposes and inclinations, but rather lives for the one who "died and was raised" for us (2 Cor. 5:15). Second is the death that as a church member coming out of the visible church he had to die in the hostile world. This second death includes without pronounced pathos the surrender even of the corporeal life, martyrdom in its more narrow sense, while martyrdom as bearing witness is already identical with every aspect of the mission.

In the New Testament these martyrdoms have nothing pathetic about them since they are the simple, logical deductions from the presupposition (admittedly pathetic) that Christian mission ultimately issues from the one who died and was raised for us. Thereby we are essentially already deprived of our rights: "None of us lives to himself, and none of us dies to himself. If we live, we live to the Lord, and if we die, we die to the Lord" (Rom. 14:7–8a). Paul expressly blocks every attempt at escape into a private existence: "Whether we live or whether we die, we are the Lord's. For to this end Christ died and lived again, that he might be Lord both of the dead and of the living" (vv. 8b–9). This lordly existence and lordly sending are described to us again when the ascension of Christ "above all the heavens" signifies the "place" from which he dispenses all missions. In the course of this it is significantly decreed that the rising above all presupposes the descent beneath all (Eph. 4:7–11). It can also be said that God exalted him above all because he had humbled himself in his mission into deepest humiliation (Phil. 2:6–11).

How it may turn out for the commissioned sheep among the wolves is not hard to imagine. That antagonism and murderous thoughts await the commissioned Christians appears self-evident to them because they are in his service—and they may expect no other fate than his. "If they persecuted me, they will persecute you" (John 15:20b). The servant is not "above his master; it is enough for . . . the servant [to be] like his master" (Matt. 10:24–25). Indeed, there is for Jesus a self-evident intensification: "If they have called the master of the house Beelzebul, how much more will they malign those of his household" (Matt. 10:25). That Peter was crucified "inverted," with his head upside down, is a clear symbol of this nonpathetic "all the more."

Today as never before in its history the church lives in

the legacy of persecution, and one can probably say that the more it is actually the church the more this is true. But because the church in its long history has persecuted others, perhaps as the persecuted it must atone for much that it has been guilty of.

There is nevertheless also the pure realm where the church stands in true discipleship. And ever since the Acts of the Apostles it knows that this being persecuted at the same time guarantees its fruitfulness in mission. There is something like a eucharistic blood bath in which its own flesh and blood—is it not the body of Christ?—are nourishment for the life of the world.

Here we push forward to the center of the mystery of the church. Because now there is nothing more to say, whether the church lives more toward death or more out of death, whether the church stands before the cross and goes to it or lives in the grace of the resurrected one with death behind in the new eternal life. Both stand unexpectedly next to one another. "If then you have been raised with Christ, seek the things that are above, where Christ is, seated at the right hand of God. . . . You have *died,* and your life is hid with Christ in God. . . . Put to death therefore what is earthly in you. . . . And whatever you do, in word or deed, do everything in the name of the Lord Jesus, giving thanks to God the Father through him" (Col. 3:1, 3, 5, 17). That is, give thanks. Dying as well as being raised obligates one to the deadening of purely earthly concerns and to a life in the Christian mission, which is always a eucharistic life.

Ultimately Good Friday, with the Good Saturday of death in itself, and Easter, with its motion toward the ascension to the Father, are inextricably intertwined in the life of the church as in the individual believer.

From Easter the believer is guided into Good Friday, emerging from the death of baptism into the eucharistic life out of death and, still further, life unto death. The Christian cannot conceive of it, but he also does not want to. It suffices to believe in the trustworthiness of the Lord, that from out of his eternal life he chose and experienced temporal death in order to confer upon the death that indwells every transitory life a new, deeper life of revalued meaning: the meaning of trinitarian devotion (which is the highest life) that in the life of Christ and in his disciples assumes the form of ignominious death. "Refuse of the world," the "offscouring" of "all things" that wish to vindicate themselves by us (1 Cor. 4:13). But precisely this ignominious death serves to purify the world.

# III

## THOROUGHLY UNITED THROUGH
## DEATH

Everything said leads to the mystery of the communion of the saints. As Paul told us, the living have died with the Lord who died for them in order to live hidden with the resurrected in God (Col. 3:3), beyond their mortality which death still has "before" them. The dead, however, who have it "behind" them, live, as Jesus tells us, as "children of the resurrection" with "the God of Abraham and the God of Isaac and the God of Jacob. Now he is not God of the dead, but of the living; for all live to him" (Luke 20:37b–38a). How should those who are "with Christ" (Phil. 1:23) not likewise be with us, since he is with us eucharistically? Death appears to us like a barrier that keeps us at a distance from heaven. Is the barrier removed? Then why should heaven not be with the earth? Accordingly, why worry about the way to heaven?

When the earthly church celebrates the Eucharist, it invokes heavenly inhabitants in the "Communicantes" prayer. In the "Memento" prayer, however, it invokes heaven itself, calling to remembrance heavenly participation in temporal events.[1] For being-for-itself, conditioned here below by mortality, has given way to the true, personal, trinitarian "being-for-others" in heaven. And it is not only the Lord of the church who died for us that trains us in dying but also everything together with him that has passed over into "life-out-of-death." From earth to heaven there is distance (already secretly overcome): from heaven to earth there is none. The hundred and forty-four thousand, whose song sounds "like the sound of many waters and like the sound of loud thunder . . . and like the sound of harpers playing on their harps" and who "follow the Lamb wherever he goes" (Rev. 14:2, 4), are just as much like those who follow him from life into death as those who follow him from death into life. And they actually follow him. So even the first band already stands under the law of life and death for all the others, and both bands travel the same path. The shepherd of the sheep "goes before them, and the sheep follow him, for they know his voice" (John 10:4).

The mysteries of the communion of the saints are as unfathomable as those of the Eucharist. Everyone who belongs to the community *has* only in order to *give,* and receives only through giving. Personality and community increase with and through one another. The paradox that "from him who has not, even what he has will

1. The "Communicantes" is a prayer early in the Roman Canon of the Mass, invoking the saints. The "Memento" invokes God's blessing upon the living church communicants.—TRANS.

be taken away'' while to the one who has the ten talents the eleventh is given (Matt. 25:28-29) astonishes no one here. In Christ's church one has only in order to give and is enriched thereby. Already on earth, mission constituted the unique, unmistakable personality of the individual Christian as much as his gifts that were to be exercised within the community of the saints.

In this double-sided account of the mission, living and dying seem to merge into one another as if transfigured. But this only under the condition that we not forget into which darknesses the devoted life must enter in order to overcome the resistance against love: "The light shines in the darkness, and the darkness has not overcome it. . . . He came to his own home, and his own people received him not" (John 1:5, 11). In this shining-in-darkness the light must forget itself in order to become "a hammer which breaks the rocks in pieces" (Jer. 23:29)—rocks that obstruct and resist the flowing communion of the saints and that only the power of suffering and dying clears out of the way.

But the rock of death ("who will roll away the stone for us?") does not defy every assault, "for love is strong as death" and the chaotic flood "cannot quench" it (Song of Solomon 8:6f.). So finally no one knows until his death how much his mission will still demand of him before he can enter into the eternal life of the communion of the saints beyond his always deepening death.